Let Those With Ears...

By

Dr. Lydia A. Woods

†††
CWP

Channing and Watt Publishers
Atlanta, GA

Channing and Watt Publishers
75 Gammon Ave SE Apt #A
Atlanta, Georgia 30315
www.channingandwatt.com

Front Cover Photo and Cover Design by
Jacqueline D. Woods/JD Woods Consulting

Back Cover Photo by
Elizabeth J. Jackson

First Edition, Copyright © 1998 Lydia A. Woods
Second Edition, Copyright © 2014 Lydia A. Woods

Printed in the United States of America

ISBN-13: 978-1-941200-16-2
LCCN: 2001088528

Other Publications
by Dr. Lydia A. Woods

Acceptance with Joy
Poems by Revelation
For the Edification of the Saints
Food for Saints
Conversations with the Saints
All the Saints Agree
Those Bible Characters
Lessons of a Handmaiden
The Movies: Their Spiritual Messages
The Joy of the Lord
Under the Rainbow

Dedicated to
My Spiritual Sisters
Delores, Terry, Gloria, Marie,
Regina, and Colleen

Acknowledgements

A piece of creative work is usually produced in isolation, but the distribution for others to see and appreciate takes many hearts and hands and minds. I want to give thanks to my friends and family members who are those hearts which support and lift me up and forward.

Special thanks to William C. Terry, Yehonatan Meru, and Veronica Norris for taking their time to proofread this book.

My appreciation to the host of colleagues, students and fellow Christian brothers and sisters who praise and encourage me and constantly remind me of the work God can do in a willing but frightened and fragile vessel.

Thank you Holy Spirit for using my humble vessel
and letting me put my name on these words.

Introduction

Under the inspiration of the Holy Spirit, I began writing Christian Poetry. When I look back at the beginning, I realize now that I knew very little about the Holy Spirit and His relationship to me. At first, I would be awakened during the night, out of a sound sleep, with a poem forming in my head, or sometimes while driving, or in the midst of conversation with someone.

I would tell people that the Spirit would come and go, then months later return, to give me poems. My understanding has since grown, and I now know that the Spirit never leaves and is always present with me and in me and thru me – the two of us are one.

I believe the Holy Spirit, is God and that God exists in every human being. The real gift of life is discovering God within you, which first blesses you, then those around you.

These collections of poems are inspired by the lessons which the Lord has been teaching me as I walk with Him. Many poems are inspired by uplifting and stimulating conversations with God's precious Saints and others are born out of the frustration that many do not know the Love of God and His amazing grace and mercy.

In reading, I hope you will find poems which speak to your heart, express what you have experienced, or have enlightened your understanding. The writing of these poems allow me an outlet of spiritual expression, as the Lord tempers and prepares me for my Calling.

Table of Contents

Poems

Answer to Many a Prayer 1
Blood Disguise 3
Boys Into Men 5
The Building You Call Church 7
Don't Forsake the Assembly 8
E.T. 9
Fruit Trees 11
Generations in You 14
The Gift 15
Has Done, Is Doing or Will Do 17
Holy Rollers 19
Jesus Learned Obedience 21
Just Give It! 25
Liar, Liar 27
My God Isn't Stupid! 31
Not in a Place Called Church 32
Obedience the Highest Form of Praise 33
The Perfect Murder 35
Resistance is Futile 37
So Great a Cloud of Witnesses 39
The U.P.S. Man 43
Upside Down, Inside Out 44
With His Own Blood 45

Scriptural References

Answer to Many a Prayer 49
Blood Disguise.. 50
Boys Into Men... 51
The Building You Call Church... 52
Don't Forsake the Assembly 53
E.T. 54
Fruit Trees 55
Generations in You 56
The Gift... 57
Has Done, Is Doing or Will Do 58
Holy Rollers 59
Jesus Learned Obedience... 60
Just Give It!... 61
Liar, Liar.. 62
My God Isn't Stupid! 63
Not in a Place Called Church... 64
Obedience the Highest Form of Praise............................... 65
The Perfect Murder.. 66
Resistance is Futile.. 67
So Great a Cloud of Witnesses.. 69
The U.P.S. Man 70
Upside Down, Inside Out 71
With His Own Blood.. 73

Scriptural Index.. 74

Poems

Dr. Lydia A. Woods

Answer to Many a Prayer

John 16:33; Romans 5:3, 12:12 (KJV)

Trials and tribulations are the answer,
To many a prayer,
You probably don't want to believe this,
But I truly swear,

That in many cases this really,
Is absolutely true,
You know in your heart,
That I'm being straight with you.

Don't pray to take,
The trials and tribulations away,
The old folk say, pray for strength,
To endure them day by day.

Those trials and tribulations are tools,
Used to shape and mold,
For He who began a good work,
Finishes, it I am told.

The potter molds the clay,
With tribulations and trials,
Knowing it can be painful,
For just a little while.

-1-

Think of trials and tribulations,
As the potters hands,
They love and caress you,
As He accomplishes His plans.

In many of those prayers you ask,
For great wisdom and knowledge,
Not the kind you get,
From attending a fancy college.

You ask – Lord make me,
Loving, and ever so kind,
Make me a giver, a good steward,
Lord give me Your mind!

I want gentleness and understanding,
And discipline for sure,
And the most sought after of all,
Is faith to endure.

Well, all of these prayers,
Can be answered just so,
Trials and tribulations my dears,
Takes care of them all – Didn't You Know!

Dr. Lydia A. Woods

Blood Disguise

Ephesians 1:7; Acts 20:28; Hebrews 9:22 (KJV)

Imagine God looking down,
From Heaven and on His face a frown.

Because He is only able to look,
Upon that which has no sin -- It's in the book!

So how does He look upon me?
So full of sin, I know His eyes will not see,

The very person who I want to be,
Holy, pure, righteous and sin free.

"Don't worry," He said, to me,
I've provided a way so you – I can see,

Just cover yourself in my Son's blood,
Which unites us together in perfect love.

For the Blood of My Son covers sin,
And now my children are able to come in.

To the presence of My Holy eyes,
Under this precious Blood Disguise!

-3-

Boys Into Men

Isaiah 54:13; Hebrews 12:6; Revelation 3:19 (KJV)

In the name of Love, parents can commit great sin,
Doing good to their children, that's when trouble begins!

With that misguided love, of helping them out,
You can ruin a good child, without a doubt.

Even though our Father can give us all we desire,
He withholds it, to save us from hell's fire.

So when I became a single parent, to three young men,
I'll share this conversation, I had with the Lord then.

Lord only You know how to make, boys into men,
I'm turning them over to You, so please begin.

He spoke to my heart and said, this to me,
"You must stay out of My way, wait on Me and see."

For what I'm about to do, will turn you inside out,
But I'll make men of your boys, never have a doubt.

Through the years He has reminded me, of how we began,
Me trusting in His knowledge, of how to make a man.

He knows just how to mold, that boy into a man,
He knows how to shape a girl, into a woman with His hand

Now here is the secret, be sharp or you will miss,
The wisdom in these next lines, will surely assist.

First and last – parents get out of the Lord's way,
'Cause it's painful to see your child suffer, even a little today.

But remember that the suffering, will strengthen that back,
God won't kill or maim them, that's a guaranteed fact!

Don't give that money, even though you have plenty,
Don't let them move back in, even if there's room for many.

Don't buy that car, or loan that money -- Not today!
Don't pay for that college, or credit card – No way!

You'll look like the bad guy, you surely can bet.
But suck it in – be tough – 'cause you'll never regret.

You didn't create a monster, that turns on you with its hate,
You didn't handicap your son or daughter, before it was too late.

That you allowed the Lord, to make your, boy into a man,
And that girl into a woman, able to on her own stand.

You'll be proud one day, of the fine job the Lord did,
That He made a Man or Woman, out of your precious Kid!

The Building You Call Church

Colossians 1:18; Matthew 16:18; Ephesians 5:27 (KJV)

It's Sunday morning and I'm going to church!
How impossible a thought this is to me.

The church is not a building,
It's not a place to go.
The church is people,
Saints, I know – You know.

The Church is the bride of our Lord,
He loves her with His life,
The Church is preparing herself,
Spot and wrinkle free to be His holy wife.

You are the building not made with hands,
A place for the Spirit of God to dwell,
It's very important to get this right,
And of course, saints, you know, I'm going to tell.

Because if you see yourself as God sees you,
Engaged to be a wife to His Son,
A temple fit to hold His precious Spirit,
You'll begin to see that God's victory is won.

Don't assign your birthright to a building,
That can do no earthly good,
That can't carry the Spirit of the Living God,
To a hurting world as it should.

So get up every morning, not just Sunday,
Let me hear these words, just say,
I'm going to take the Church this morning,
And minister to a hurting world today!

-7-

Don't Forsake the Assembly

Hebrews 10:25; Matthew 18:20 (KJV)

To me this is the most abused phrase,
In the Book.
I'm tired of the usage,
Just to get people hooked.

To keep them in bondage,
To keep them coming back,
You know it's your duty,
So don't be slack!

Tell me where it says that,
This phrase really means
On Sunday morning and Wednesday evening,
Every saint should be seen,

Assembling together for the purpose,
Of worship or to edify,
I'm just asking a simple question,
Please tell me why?

My Book says, "where two or three are gathered,"
He will be there.
It never says,
When, how many times or even where.

If I am missing the point,
Please set me straight,
'Cause man's traditions,
Really give me a huge headache!

E.T.

(E.T. – The Movie) John 14:1-4 (KJV)

You've all seen the movie,
But what you didn't see,
Is that E.T. looks,
A lot like you and me.

Now he was left on earth,
By those he loved.
And he searched for their return,
In the heavens above.

I'm sure he volunteered,
To be part of the crew,
To complete the task,
That they came to earth to do.

But the job got a little complex,
And scary towards the end.
He didn't bargain for all the trouble,
That befell him.

Phone home E.T.,
So your people will know,
That you have had enough of earth,
And you are ready to go!

They pursued you and sought,
To take your life,
Why did they leave you here,
With all this strife?

What lessons have you learned,
In your brief stay,
You met some gentle and loving people,
Along the way.

But what about those others,
Who were full of fear,
Because of your difference,
You became a threat here.

But you left your mark,
And touched some souls,
You showed them love,
The young and the old.

Your purpose completed,
They did come back for you,
And you were changed,
By this earthly experience too.

The spiritual message in that film,
Speaks to you and me,
For this strange place earth,
Is grievous you see,

Lord I identify with E.T.,
And long to be,
Back home with You,
In Eternity!

E.T.   *A Collection of Christian Poems*

Fruit Trees

Galatians 5:22-23 (KJV)

There's much talk about fruit,
In the Bible, you know.
But not the kind that in a garden,
You can grow.

Can't pick it,
From a plant or bush or tree,
Or find it,
In your neighborhood grocery.

Now there are nine kinds,
Of fruit for your delight,
But you can't see them,
With your natural sight.

And they are planted,
In the oddest place, you know,
In the heart of humans,
Is where this fruit will grow.

For humans are the tree,
So the Word of God tells,
Where all the potential,
For this fruit to grow dwells.

And you can tell,
If the tree is good,
And if the fruit is growing,
As it should.

Now these nine kinds of fruit,
Let me remind,
Are love, joy and peace,
Just one of a kind.

Also long-suffering, gentleness,
Goodness and faith,
Meekness, and temperance,
All in their place.

They all grow from one tree,
Now that seems strange.
But the heart of a reborn human,
Has been rearranged.

By the Spirit of God,
Who is seed for this amazing tree,
Let these nine precious fruit grow,
In abundance in you and me.

Now pass out,
Your fruit every day,
To those you meet,
Along life's way.

Make sure the fruit,
Is fresh and pure,
For the substance of life,
In this fruit will endure,

The evils of this world,
And prevail over the wicked one,
And bring us safely home,
When the job is done!

Generations in You

Psalm 127:3-5, 128:3 (KJV)

I have so many desires and dreams,
This life isn't long enough it seems.

For me to fulfill all that I want to do,
It's frustrating for me to attempt to.

But the Lord explained it to me just so,
So that I wouldn't get too anxious, you know.

That in all my dreams and desires,
Is just the vision of generations inspired.

The deeds of my children, grandchildren and more,
Lay in me, for I am just a door.

To the future of all that God has planned,
To accomplish through me by His loving hand.

So don't regret what you didn't become,
It will happen in a grandchild, or daughter or son.

You didn't sacrifice your life in vain for the kids,
That famous painter, or athlete in future will live.

My soul is at peace,
My footsteps have been ordered by Him,
I look forward to the fulfillment in them.

All my dreams, I will fulfill through my seed,
This is God's amazing fantastic plan indeed!

Dr. Lydia A. Woods

The Gift

Psalm 111:10; Proverbs 16:16-25 (KJV)

Wisdom is the gift,
You want to give away,
But nobody seems to want it,
In this present day.

It's a valuable thing,
You'll pay a precious price,
It costs blood, sweat and tears,
And a piece of your life!

Not money, or silver,
Not even gold,
Can buy this precious thing,
Possessed by the old.

The old one wishes to make a gift,
To the young,
To friends and family,
To daughters and sons.

But no one seems,
To want to take it free,
They all choose to buy their own,
So let them be.

-15-

Let them pay,
With their own blood, sweat, and tears,
For to pay for that thing,
Called wisdom could take years.

So in buying your wisdom,
Buy this too,
That you can't give it to just anyone,
Only those who,

God sends to you,
Now you can give it away.
But hold tight,
To the wisdom until that day.

The giving is usually not to children,
Relatives, or friends
But a stranger who crosses your path,
Every now and then.

And with wisdom you'll begin,
To recognize,
Just who of those strangers,
Will cherish the prize!

Has Done, Is Doing or Will Do

Psalm 71:15, 35:28, 40:5; Job 9:10 (KJV)

I have a sister in the Lord,
That lives at a distance from me.
It's a long distance call,
So I use nine cents a minute, 'cause it ain't free.

So we can't call often,
And when we do there's quite a need,
For a Saint who knows the Word,
And has revelation on what they read.

And sometimes that need is just to report,
About what He has done, is doing or will do.
Now here's the thing that struck me the other day,
When the call was done and we were through.

You know a strange thing seems to happen,
I've noticed every time, without fail,
That my feet no longer touch the ground,
And for the time being Satan is back in hell.

Just to talk about the Lord,
What He has done, is doing or will do,
Delights and thrills His soul,
And He takes pleasure in me and you.

And we are both edified and strengthened,
And ready to face the trials ahead.
Where two or more are gathered in His name,
Is much deeper than at first I read.

There's a blessing to be found,
Just to speak about His Word,
What He has done, is doing or will do,
This is revelation I've never heard.

So keep the conversation about others,
And negative things far from you,
Invest in bragging on the Lord,
What He has done, is doing or will do!

Dr. Lydia A. Woods

Holy Rollers

I Peter 1:23, 2:9; John 1:12-13; I John 5:1 (KJV)

In downtown Chicago,
On street corners you'll see,
Men ranting, repent,
Jesus loves you and me.

Quoting scriptures, dirty clothes,
Unshaven, not clean.
They make you think serving God,
Is a crazy man's thing.

It makes you afraid,
'Cause it's quite extreme.
To be avoided at all cost,
You know what I mean.

Then there are those,
We used to call "Holy Roller" types,
In church all day long,
And into the nights.

Every other word from their mouth,
Is, "Thank You Lord,"
And all they can talk about,
Is the Jesus they adore.

I never wanted those,
"Holy Rollers" to bother me,
Cause they talked so strange,
I just wanted to flee!

But when I got saved,
A funny thing happened to me,
My eyes were opened,
And I began to see.

My ears could hear,
And I lost the fear,
And any testimony of the Lord,
And His Word I loved to hear.

And I'll talk about Him if you let me,
Night and day,
And I'll talk to anyone interested,
In what I have to say.

Now it has occurred to me,
What the Lord has secretly done.
One of those "Holy Rollers,"
I have without a doubt become!

Jesus Learned Obedience

Hebrews 5:8 (KJV)

Obedience is learned –
Not something that happens suddenly,
It isn't automatic,
It's earned, not free.

If you are raising children,
You know what I mean,
Teaching lessons over and over,
Can cause many a scene!

Why don't children just learn,
The first time that we teach,
But they get mad at us,
And say – all we do is preach,

About cleaning their rooms,
And washing the dishes,
They accuse us of never,
Considering their wishes.

And we know their wishes,
Are to play and play,
To eat our food,
And spend our money every day.

Being with their friends,
And having a good time,
Is all that they ever have,
On their minds.

-21-

Their flesh is not designed,
To heed our words about chores.
They think we come from another planet –
Just very big bores!

Their flesh is not designed,
To bow to our will,
Do you ever get this comment,
"Mom or dad – just chill!,"

If you want to understand,
How we treat God?
See the similarities between our children –
It isn't so odd!

Let's face it Saints,
We want to have it our own way,
We don't want to heed,
What the Lord has to say!

He sounds like an alien,
From outer space,
His Words are too hard,
To endure in this place.

Who wants to learn obedience,
It takes too much time.
And this suffering thing,
Are you out of your mind!

Take that suffering thing,
Somewhere else,
I'm getting over in this life,
I'm out for myself.

But out for myself,
Is not what it's all about,
That's a short-lived trip,
Without a doubt.

Jesus suffered obedience,
For all mankind,
Boy! He must have been completely,
Out of His mind!

Dr. Lydia A. Woods

Just Give It!

Acts 20:35; Luke 6:34-38 (KJV)

A borrower nor,
A lender be,
Just a giver,
Cause it makes you free.

Free from violating,
Your Father's Word.
And honoring the teaching,
That you have heard.

There's bondage in borrowing,
From a friend.
Or a neighbor or bank,
And especially your kin.

Have you noticed that things tend,
To get in the way,
Trying to make it impossible,
For that debt to pay.

And when you are the lender,
Things are going on there,
Cause you're expecting your money back,
Just your fair share.

They said they would pay,
And you took it for true,
Now they can't be found –
Are they avoiding you?

-25-

Now resentment for that person,
Is building in your heart,
Because there was good and pure,
Intentions on your part.

Now there is a mess,
Between friends or your kin,
And both of you have fallen,
So easily into sin,

They had every intention,
Of paying it back,
Why does it always happen,
That they get sidetracked?

Now that's the wisdom,
In the Word you see,
And these kinds of problems,
Need never be.

Me mad at you,
And you resenting me,
Just give it!
Honor the Word, and be Free!

Dr. Lydia A. Woods

Liar, Liar

II Timothy 2:11; Romans 6:3-4 (KJV)

Liar, Liar,
Pants on fire,
Can't pee as high,
As a telephone wire!

You remember this one,
From back in the day,
When you and your friends,
Were outside at play.

Remember the whoppers,
You told back then,
Your were only being creative,
It wasn't a sin.

But put away those childish things,
Now my dear,
I call you to truth,
Be honest and sincere.

When you say that you've given,
Your life to Christ,
Engaged to the bridegroom,
And hope to be His wife.

-27-

A Collection of Christian Poems *Liar, Liar*

Now be careful here 'cause this,
Is the important part,
Remember you can't keep even a small piece.
Of your heart.

Every body part, thought,
Deed and desire,
Everything in life,
That you have acquired.

The day you gave,
Your heart to Him,
It was only about two percent of you,
My friend!

That gets you in the game,
Now you're ready to play,
I'm telling you the truth,
About your salvation day!

The Lord wants every bit and part,
All of you,
But even you can't give you,
Like you want to,

Dr. Lydia A. Woods

Cause you're not suicidal,
And you love your life,
You're not giving it up,
Without a fight.

And a fight is what you're going to get,
In this new walk,
Do a couple of rounds with Satan,
Then let's hear you talk.

You start giving,
That life up bit by bit,
There are many times,
You think to quit.

But you know you can only go,
Forward from here,
So you strive to be closer to the One,
You love so dear.

The One who can,
Cut a raw diamond to clear perfection,
The Father who gives us,
Much loving, needed correction.

The One who helps the baby grow,
Into a woman or man.
The potter who molds and remolds,
With His skilful hands.

The One who breaks the wild horse,
So it's fit to ride,
The One who will never ever,
Leave your side.

So don't be,
In denial today,
Just keep giving Him your life,
In every way.

And don't be ignorant,
Of what He has begun,
He's out for all of you,
And He'll not lose even one!

Dr. Lydia A. Woods

My God Isn't Stupid!

Genesis 2:8-9 (KJV)

Concrete cities designed to kill,
Destroy gardens, trees, and mountainous hills.

Man thrives in a garden you know,
So to kill him place him where nothing will grow.

There is no life in concrete and stone.
Definitely no place for flesh and bone.

Tiny living spaces stacked very high,
Crowded together and do you know why?

A master plan to destroy the seed,
Who is capable of this dreadful deed?

The wicked one destroys, kills, and steals,
It's a simple plan and Satan is for real.

Look how man has fallen for this evil plan.
Destroying the earth and water, forest and land.

Hunting animals to extinction, polluting the air,
It could make one worry or even despair.

But there is a time appointed by the Holy One,
We must always remember,
That the victory is already won.

In this latter day it looks like we'll all regret,
But like I always say, My God isn't Stupid!

-31-

Not in a Place Called Church

II Peter 2:1-3; II Timothy 2:15; II Corinthians 6:16 (KJV)

Saints, I'll not have you ignorant.

Of the many voices,
And teachings in the world today,
It's big business to say "I've come in His name,"
And lead many a flock astray.

For their doctrines are filled with vanity and proof,
Clouding your mind and the Word's very truth.
If you are not schooled in the Word you'll believe,
That a preacher is gifted and you'll follow their lead.

You must study to show yourself approved and equipped,
To judge what you hear so you will not slip,
Into following the many voices in the air,
And every wind of doctrine – Please, Saints beware.

Precious Saints never follow any man's lead.
For the Word is within and that's all you need.
Don't get caught worshipping the creature.
For Jesus sent the Comforter as your only teacher.

You won't find Him in a place called "Church," not today!
But in a place not made with hands the scriptures say.
That place lies within the human heart,
Now isn't that one of our many body parts?

Know ye not that your body is the temple in this day,
Go there to seek the Lord and hear Him say,
All that you need to know and understand,
About your purpose and how to live as He commands.

Dr. Lydia A. Woods

Obedience the Highest Form of Praise

Hebrews 5:8; Romans 5:19; Philippians 2:8 (KJV)

Raise your hands in the congregation,
And call it praise!

Pray in many glorious words,
And call it praise!

Sing in your most beautiful voice,
And call it praise!

Dress in your finest apparel,
And call it Praise!

Play loudly on fine instruments,
And call it Praise!

Build the finest buildings,
And call it Praise!

Meet often with the Saints,
And call it Praise!

Work in your churches,
And call it Praise!

Obedience is the highest form, of Praise I know.
Obedience is frankly, the only route to go.
What is this obedience, that she is talking about?
Make it clear to me, without a doubt!

Jesus learned obedience, by the things that He suffered.
Now what are these things, that are used for buffers?
Things that make you want, to run away in fear.
Things that are not pleasing, to your flesh, my dears.

Things that don't make sense, to your mind.
Things that literally kick you, in the behind.
Things that you know, he told only to you.
Things that are against what family, wants you to do.

Things that will cause you, grief and pain.
Things that will make you feel, a little deranged.
Things that you won't run out, and do right away.
Things that take time and suffering before you'll say.

Lord, I will gladly do it, because I've conquered the fear,
And finally I see clearly, my purpose here.
I must voluntarily lose my life to gain it, for that is your plan.
This sometimes takes a lifetime, to understand.

My life and my will I'll fight, to the death to keep.
But it's to the death, that I freely give it to God, so I can reap.
The greatest reward, that obedience can possibly win,
Is to reign with His Son in eternity – Free from Sin!

The Perfect Murder

Romans 7:14-21 (KJV)

The perfect murder, I plot at night,
My enemy to put permanently out of sight!

It has ruined my life, so it must go,
I'm talking about my *Will* – you know.

I've tried to kill it many times before,
I've kicked it to the curb and out the door.

It won't stay dead or get in line.
But maybe it *Will* stay dead this time!

'Cause this time, I'm giving it up to the One,
Whose dealt with *Will* since times begun.

Since killing it is not the way,
I'll give it to God each and every day.

It's not killing that He has in mind,
But little adjustments made over time.

He's slowly lining it up with His own will,
'Cause a *Will* is something you just can't kill!

Dr. Lydia A. Woods

Resistance is Futile

I Corinthians 6:17, 12:12-27 (KJV)

Resistance is futile,
Trekkies know just what I mean.
The Borg is coming,
And it's a hopeless, frightening thing.

Wherever they go,
The purpose is clear.
To assimilate – and resistance,
Is futile, my dear.

Well that was Hollywood's version,
Of the way it ought to be,
But if you understand the plot,
I know you will see.

That the Borg's plan isn't original,
They took their cue,
From the master planner,
Who is assimilating me and you.

　　　　　　　　　　Resistance is Futile

Now if you resist – you remember,
The consequence of the Borg,
Either assimilate or be destroyed,
The choice is all yours.

Individual entities,
With one collective mind,
Working for an evil purpose,
To destroy all life forms and humankind.

Now the collective mind of God,
Is just the opposite you see,
To give eternal life to humankind,
And to set them forever free.

Free from evil, death and sin –
Please assimilate me now!
I will not put up a fight,
Because Resistance is Futile!

So Great a Cloud of Witnesses

Hebrews 12:1 (KJV)

Now that great cloud of witnesses,
Is watching as you run.
This race that's set before you,
Filled with hazards and hurdles,
Not quite my idea of fun.

I got a mental picture,
As I talked with a Saint the other day,
Of the size and number of the hurdles,
That we encounter along the way.

I was describing my life,
In racing terms of course,
I had just taken a big hurdle,
Caught my foot and hit the turf.

Now I'm lying on the track.
Scraped knees, bleeding hands, wounded pride,
And I look to the left,
As runners pass me right in stride.

I lay there for a moment,
Waiting for assistance from on High,
I'm moaning and groaning nursing my wounds,
And feeling like I might as well just die.

But death is not in the picture,
'Cause that's the easy way out.
I'm expected to pick myself up,
Take joy in my affliction, without doubt,

That I'm going to make it to the end,
Of this lifelong race that's set out for me.
Running hurdles in the dark,
With only faith to carry me.

But besides the faith to finish,
Just remember the league you're in,
For that Great Cloud of Witnesses,
Is cheering for your success to win.

And I heard that Cloud of Witnesses,
Just the other day.
As I pulled myself up from another fall,
And was stewing in my dismay.

That Cloud of Witnesses was great.
The number I couldn't quite make out.
And they were cheering rather loudly,
As if I was winning without a doubt.

I realized at that moment,
That it didn't matter the shape I was in,
'Cause this race is not about strong or swift,
But enduring to the end.

Endurance isn't pretty,
Cause every mark has a tale to tell.
Of the battles with Satan,
In the very depths of hell.

But it's about the race,
And the cleansing process along the way.
So that we can stand without spot or blemish,
In His presence on that Day!

The U.P.S. Man

John 4:44; Psalm 105:15 (KJV)

Do you get mad at the UPS man
When he delivers your package into your hands?

If you don't like what's delivered to you,
Notify the sender that's what you do.

Now that's all a prophet does you see,
Delivers messages from God to you and me.

But a prophet is not liked in their own land,
Cause being prophetic is not in high demand.

It's not easy being a prophet, speaking what God has to say,
To a rebellious people, not so different than back in the day.

If the news is good, please tell me more,
But keep bad news to yourself, or just hit the door.

So just treat a prophet like the UPS guy,
Thank them kindly, close the door, cause this is why,

The UPS man didn't send that package to you,
If you have a problem with it, You know Who to take it to!

-43-

Upside Down, Inside Out

Romans 1:21-32 (KJV)

Make no mistake about it,
We're living in the time of the end.
Everything is upside down and inside out,
It doesn't seem like we can win.

Don't feel sorry for the victim,
'Cause the crook's a battered child.
Violence all around us,
Homosexuality right in style.

Compassion seems nonexistent,
Keep hustling to get ahead.
The pressure is tremendous,
Folk's jumping from bed to bed.

Killing babies, hurting children,
Homelessness and hunger in your face.
Rapidly heading for destruction,
Will there be no winners in this race?

The race is not given to the swift or the strong,
But time is running out, where is the end?
Upside down and Inside out,
Lord Jesus, deliver us from this world of sin!

Dr. Lydia A. Woods

With His Own Blood

Acts 20:28; Hosea 2:19; Revelation 19:7-9, 21:9 (KJV)

I love a love story,
As most women do.
Give me a happy ending,
Plus boxes of tissue too.

I'll cry you a bucket,
In the dark of any show.
'Cause a love story pulls,
At my heartstrings, anyway it goes.

Well the greatest love story ever written,
I know of in this life,
Is the love of Jesus Christ for the church,
His sought after wife.

The most romantic thing I know,
Is a man laying down His life,
For the woman that He loves,
For His precious, beloved wife.

The horrible death that He suffered,
So that His beloved could only live.
Is the most beautiful gift of love,
That anyone can give.

My favorite hymn ever,
I've loved it since a child.
The melody sweetly haunts me,
As I hum the tune awhile.

-45-

"From heaven He came and sought her,
To be His holy bride,
With His own blood He bought her,
And for her life He died.*"

But not like Romeo and Juliet,
Star-crossed lovers in that tale,
That only in death,
Can they together dwell.

Our love story is unsurpassed,
For not even death can hold,
This lover in the grave,
That's how this love story goes.

The ending tells,
Of the greatest victory won,
For God so loved the world,
He gave His only Son.

After giving up His life,
For His beloved precious Bride,
He is raised again to life,
And awaits her by His Side!

* "The Church's One Foundation" By Samuel J. Stone and Samuel S. Wesley

Scriptural References

Answer to Many a Prayer

John 16:33; Romans 5:3, 12:12 (KJV)

John 16:33 (KJV)

33 These things I have spoken unto you, that in me ye might have peace. In the world ye shall have tribulation: but be of good cheer; I have overcome the world.

Romans 5:3 (KJV)

3 And not only so, but we glory in tribulations also: knowing that tribulation worketh patience;

Romans 12:12 (KJV)

12 Rejoicing in hope; patient in tribulation; continuing instant in prayer;

Blood Disguise

Ephesians 1:7; Acts 20:28; Hebrews 9:22 (KJV)

Ephesians 1:7 (KJV)
7 In whom we have redemption through his blood, the forgiveness of sins, according to the riches of his grace;

Acts 20:28 (KJV)
28 Take heed therefore unto yourselves, and to all the flock, over the which the Holy Ghost hath made you overseers, to feed the church of God, which he hath purchased with his own blood.

Boys Into Men

Isaiah 54:13; Hebrews 12:6; Revelation 3:19 (KJV)

Isaiah 54:13 (KJV)
13 And all thy children shall be taught of the LORD; and great shall be the peace of thy children.

Hebrews 12:6 (KJV)
6 For whom the Lord loveth he chasteneth, and scourgeth every son whom he receiveth.

Revelation 3:19 (KJV)
19 As many as I love, I rebuke and chasten: be zealous therefore, and repent.

The Building You Call Church

Colossians 1:18; Matthew 16:18; Ephesians 5:27 (KJV)

Colossians 1:18 (KJV)
18 And he is the head of the body, the church: who is the beginning, the firstborn from the dead; that in all things he might have the preeminence.

Matthew 16:18 (KJV)
18 And I say also unto thee, That thou art Peter, and upon this rock I will build my church; and the gates of hell shall not prevail against it.

Ephesians 5:27 (KJV)
27 That he might present it to himself a glorious church, not having spot, or wrinkle, or any such thing; but that it should be holy and without blemish.

Dr. Lydia A. Woods

Don't Forsake the Assembly

Hebrews 10:25; Matthew 18:20 (KJV)

Hebrews 10:25 (KJV)
25 Not forsaking the assembling of ourselves together, as the manner of some is; but exhorting one another: and so much the more, as ye see the day approaching.

Matthew 18:20 (KJV)
20 For where two or three are gathered together in my name, there am I in the midst of them.

E.T.

(E.T, the Movie) John 14:1-4 (KJV)

John 14:1-4 (KJV)

[1] Let not your heart be troubled: ye believe in God, believe also in me.

[2] In my Father's house are many mansions: if it were not so, I would have told you. I go to prepare a place for you.

[3] And if I go and prepare a place for you, I will come again, and receive you unto myself; that where I am, there ye may be also.

[4] And whither I go ye know, and the way ye know.

Fruit Trees

Galatians 5:22-23 (KJV)

Galatians 5:22-23 (KJV)
22 But the fruit of the Spirit is love, joy, peace, longsuffering, gentleness, goodness, faith,
23 Meekness, temperance: against such there is no law.

Generations in You

Psalm 127:3-5, 128:3 (KJV)

Psalm 127:3-5 (KJV)

[3] Lo, children are an heritage of the LORD: and the fruit of the womb is his reward.

[4] As arrows are in the hand of a mighty man; so are children of the youth.

[5] Happy is the man that hath his quiver full of them: they shall not be ashamed, but they shall speak with the enemies in the gate.

Psalm 128:3 (KJV)

[3] Thy wife shall be as a fruitful vine by the sides of thine house: thy children like olive plants round about thy table.

-56-

The Gift

Psalm 111:10; Proverbs 16:16-25 (KJV)

Psalm 111:10 (KJV)

10 The fear of the LORD is the beginning of wisdom: a good understanding have all they that do his commandments: his praise endureth for ever.

Proverbs 16:16-25 (KJV)

16 How much better is it to get wisdom than gold! and to get understanding rather to be chosen than silver!

17 The highway of the upright is to depart from evil: he that keepeth his way preserveth his soul.

18 Pride goeth before destruction, and an haughty spirit before a fall.

19 Better it is to be of an humble spirit with the lowly, than to divide the spoil with the proud.

20 He that handleth a matter wisely shall find good: and whoso trusteth in the LORD, happy is he.

21 The wise in heart shall be called prudent: and the sweetness of the lips increaseth learning.

22 Understanding is a wellspring of life unto him that hath it: but the instruction of fools is folly.

23 The heart of the wise teacheth his mouth, and addeth learning to his lips.

24 Pleasant words are as an honeycomb, sweet to the soul, and health to the bones.

25 There is a way that seemeth right unto a man, but the end thereof are the ways of death.

Has Done, Is Doing or Will Do

Psalm 71:15, 35:28, 40:5; Job 9:10 (KJV)

Psalm 71:15 (KJV)
15 My mouth shall shew forth thy righteousness and thy salvation all the day; for I know not the numbers thereof.

Psalm 35:28 (KJV)
28 And my tongue shall speak of thy righteousness and of thy praise all the day long.

Psalm 40:5 (KJV)
5 Many, O LORD my God, are thy wonderful works which thou hast done, and thy thoughts which are to us-ward: they cannot be reckoned up in order unto thee: if I would declare and speak of them, they are more than can be numbered.

Job 9:10 (KJV)
10 Which doeth great things past finding out; yea, and wonders without number.

Holy Rollers

I Peter 1:23, 2:9; John 1:12-13; I John 5:1 (KJV)

I Peter 1:23 (KJV)
23 Being born again, not of corruptible seed, but of incorruptible, by the word of God, which liveth and abideth for ever.

I Peter 2:9 (KJV)
9 But ye are a chosen generation, a royal priesthood, an holy nation, a peculiar people; that ye should shew forth the praises of him who hath called you out of darkness into his marvellous light;

John 1:12-13 (KJV)
12 But as many as received him, to them gave he power to become the sons of God, even to them that believe on his name:
13 Which were born, not of blood, nor of the will of the flesh, nor of the will of man, but of God.

I John 5:1 (KJV)
1 Whosoever believeth that Jesus is the Christ is born of God: and every one that loveth him that begat loveth him also that is begotten of him.

Jesus Learned Obedience

Hebrews 5:8 (KJV)

Hebrews 5:8 (KJV)

8 Though he were a Son, yet learned he obedience by the things which he suffered;

Just Give It!

Acts 20:35; Luke 6:34-38 (KJV)

Acts 20:35 (KJV)

35 I have shewed you all things, how that so labouring ye ought to support the weak, and to remember the words of the Lord Jesus, how he said, It is more blessed to give than to receive.

Luke 6:34-38 (KJV)

34 And if ye lend to them of whom ye hope to receive, what thank have ye? for sinners also lend to sinners, to receive as much again.

35 But love ye your enemies, and do good, and lend, hoping for nothing again; and your reward shall be great, and ye shall be the children of the Highest: for he is kind unto the unthankful and to the evil.

36 Be ye therefore merciful, as your Father also is merciful.

37 Judge not, and ye shall not be judged: condemn not, and ye shall not be condemned: forgive, and ye shall be forgiven:

38 Give, and it shall be given unto you; good measure, pressed down, and shaken together, and running over, shall men give into your bosom. For with the same measure that ye mete withal it shall be measured to you again.

Liar, Liar

II Timothy 2:11; Romans 6:3-4 (KJV)

II Timothy 2:11 (KJV)
[11] It is a faithful saying: For if we be dead with him, we shall also live with him:

Romans 6:3-4 (KJV)
[3] Know ye not, that so many of us as were baptized into Jesus Christ were baptized into his death?
[4] Therefore we are buried with him by baptism into death: that like as Christ was raised up from the dead by the glory of the Father, even so we also should walk in newness of life.

-62-

My God Isn't Stupid!

Genesis 2:8-9 (KJV)

Genesis 2:8-9 (KJV)

8 And the LORD God planted a garden eastward in Eden; and there he put the man whom he had formed.

9 And out of the ground made the LORD God to grow every tree that is pleasant to the sight, and good for food; the tree of life also in the midst of the garden, and the tree of knowledge of good and evil.

Not in a Place Called Church

II Peter 2:1-3; II Timothy 2:15; II Corinthians 6:16 (KJV)

II Peter 2:1-3 (KJV)
¹ But there were false prophets also among the people, even as there shall be false teachers among you, who privily shall bring in damnable heresies, even denying the Lord that bought them, and bring upon themselves swift destruction.
² And many shall follow their pernicious ways; by reason of whom the way of truth shall be evil spoken of.
³ And through covetousness shall they with feigned words make merchandise of you: whose judgment now of a long time lingereth not, and their damnation slumbereth not.

II Timothy 2:15 (KJV)
¹⁵ Study to shew thyself approved unto God, a workman that needeth not to be ashamed, rightly dividing the word of truth.

II Corinthians 6:16 (KJV)
¹⁶ And what agreement hath the temple of God with idols? for ye are the temple of the living God; as God hath said, I will dwell in them, and walk in them; and I will be their God, and they shall be my people.

Obedience the Highest Form of Praise

Hebrews 5:8; Romans 5:19; Philippians 2:8 (KJV)

Hebrews 5:8 (KJV)
8 Though he were a Son, yet learned he obedience by the things which he suffered;

Romans 5:19 (KJV)
19 For as by one man's disobedience many were made sinners, so by the obedience of one shall many be made righteous.

Philippians 2:8 (KJV)
8 And being found in fashion as a man, he humbled himself, and became obedient unto death, even the death of the cross.

The Perfect Murder

Romans 7:14-21 (KJV)

Romans 7:14-21 (KJV)

[14] For we know that the law is spiritual: but I am carnal, sold under sin.

[15] For that which I do I allow not: for what I would, that do I not; but what I hate, that do I.

[16] If then I do that which I would not, I consent unto the law that it is good.

[17] Now then it is no more I that do it, but sin that dwelleth in me.

[18] For I know that in me (that is, in my flesh,) dwelleth no good thing: for to will is present with me; but how to perform that which is good I find not.

[19] For the good that I would I do not: but the evil which I would not, that I do.

[20] Now if I do that I would not, it is no more I that do it, but sin that dwelleth in me.

[21] I find then a law, that, when I would do good, evil is present with me.

Dr. Lydia A. Woods

Resistance is Futile

I Corinthians 6:17, 12:12-27 (KJV)

I Corinthians 6:17 (KJV)
17 But he that is joined unto the Lord is one spirit.

I Corinthians 12:12-27 (KJV)
12 For as the body is one, and hath many members, and all the members of that one body, being many, are one body: so also is Christ.
13 For by one Spirit are we all baptized into one body, whether we be Jews or Gentiles, whether we be bond or free; and have been all made to drink into one Spirit.
14 For the body is not one member, but many.
15 If the foot shall say, Because I am not the hand, I am not of the body; is it therefore not of the body?
16 And if the ear shall say, Because I am not the eye, I am not of the body; is it therefore not of the body?
17 If the whole body were an eye, where were the hearing? If the whole were hearing, where were the smelling?
18 But now hath God set the members every one of them in the body, as it hath pleased him.
19 And if they were all one member, where were the body?
20 But now are they many members, yet but one body.
21 And the eye cannot say unto the hand, I have no need of thee: nor again the head to the feet, I have no need of you.
22 Nay, much more those members of the body, which seem to be more feeble, are necessary:
23 And those members of the body, which we think to be less honourable, upon these we bestow more abundant honour; and our uncomely parts have more abundant comeliness.

-67-

24 For our comely parts have no need: but God hath tempered the body together, having given more abundant honour to that part which lacked.

25 That there should be no schism in the body; but that the members should have the same care one for another.

26 And whether one member suffer, all the members suffer with it; or one member be honoured, all the members rejoice with it.

27 Now ye are the body of Christ, and members in particular.

Dr. Lydia A. Woods

So Great a Cloud of Witnesses

Hebrews 12:1 (KJV)

Hebrews 12:1 (KJV)
[1] Wherefore seeing we also are compassed about with so great a cloud of witnesses, let us lay aside every weight, and the sin which doth so easily beset us, and let us run with patience the race that is set before us,

The U.P.S. Man

John 4:44; Psalm 105:15 (KJV)

John 4:44 (KJV)
44 For Jesus himself testified, that a prophet hath no honour in his own country.

Psalm 105:15 (KJV)
15 Saying, Touch not mine anointed, and do my prophets no harm.

Dr. Lydia A. Woods

Upside Down, Inside Out

Romans 1:21-32 (KJV)

Romans 1:21-32 (KJV)

[21] Because that, when they knew God, they glorified him not as God, neither were thankful; but became vain in their imaginations, and their foolish heart was darkened.

[22] Professing themselves to be wise, they became fools,

[23] And changed the glory of the uncorruptible God into an image made like to corruptible man, and to birds, and fourfooted beasts, and creeping things.

[24] Wherefore God also gave them up to uncleanness through the lusts of their own hearts, to dishonour their own bodies between themselves:

[25] Who changed the truth of God into a lie, and worshipped and served the creature more than the Creator, who is blessed for ever. Amen.

[26] For this cause God gave them up unto vile affections: for even their women did change the natural use into that which is against nature:

[27] And likewise also the men, leaving the natural use of the woman, burned in their lust one toward another; men with men working that which is unseemly, and receiving in themselves that recompence of their error which was meet.

[28] And even as they did not like to retain God in their knowledge, God gave them over to a reprobate mind, to do those things which are not convenient;

[29] Being filled with all unrighteousness, fornication, wickedness, covetousness, maliciousness; full of envy, murder, debate, deceit, malignity; whisperers,

[30] Backbiters, haters of God, despiteful, proud, boasters, inventors of evil things, disobedient to parents,

-71-

[31] Without understanding, covenantbreakers, without natural affection, implacable, unmerciful:

[32] Who knowing the judgment of God, that they which commit such things are worthy of death, not only do the same, but have pleasure in them that do them.

With His Own Blood

Acts 20:28; Hosea 2:19; Revelation 19:7-9, 21:9 (KJV)

Acts 20:28 (KJV)
28 Take heed therefore unto yourselves, and to all the flock, over the which the Holy Ghost hath made you overseers, to feed the church of God, which he hath purchased with his own blood.

Hosea 2:19 (KJV)
19 And I will betroth thee unto me for ever; yea, I will betroth thee unto me in righteousness, and in judgment, and in lovingkindness, and in mercies.

Revelation 19:7-9 (KJV)
7 Let us be glad and rejoice, and give honour to him: for the marriage of the Lamb is come, and his wife hath made herself ready.
8 And to her was granted that she should be arrayed in fine linen, clean and white: for the fine linen is the righteousness of saints.
9 And he saith unto me, Write, Blessed are they which are called unto the marriage supper of the Lamb. And he saith unto me, These are the true sayings of God.

Revelation 21:9 (KJV)
9 And there came unto me one of the seven angels which had the seven vials full of the seven last plagues, and talked with me, saying, Come hither, I will shew thee the bride, the Lamb's wife.

Scriptural
Index

Genesis
2:8-9
  My God Isn't Stupid!, 31, 63
Job
9:10
  Has Done, Is Doing or Will Do,
  17, 58
Psalms
35:28
  Has Done, Is Doing or Will Do,
  17, 58
40:5
  Has Done, Is Doing or Will Do,
  17, 58
71:15
  Has Done, Is Doing or Will Do,
  17, 58
105:15
  The U.P.S. Man, 43, 70
111:10
  The Gift, 15, 57
127:3-5
  Generations in You, 14, 56
128:3
  Generations in You, 14, 56
Proverbs
16:16-25
  The Gift, 15, 57
Isaiah
54:13
  Boys Into Men, 5, 51
Hosea
2:19
  With His Own Blood, 45, 73
Matthew
16:18
  The Building You Call Church,
  7, 52

18:20
  Don't Forsake the Assembly, 8,
  53
Luke
6:34-38
  Just Give It!, 25, 61
John
1:12-13
  Holy Rollers, 19, 59
4:44
  The U.P.S. Man, 43, 70
14:1-4
  E.T., 9, 54
16:33
  Answer to Many a Prayer, 1, 49
Acts
20:28
  Blood Disguise, 3, 50
  With His Own Blood, 45, 73
20:35
  Just Give It!, 25, 61
Romans
1:21-32
  Upside Down, Inside Out, 44,
  71
5:3
  Answer to Many a Prayer, 1, 49
5:19
  Obedience the Highest Form of
  Praise, 33, 65
6:3-4
  Liar, Liar, 27, 62
7:14-21
  The Perfect Murder, 35, 66
12:12
  Answer to Many a Prayer, 1, 49
I Corinthians
6:17
  Resistance is Futile, 37, 67

A Collection of Christian Poems   *Scriptural Index*

12:12-27
Resistance is Futile, 37, 67
II Corinthians
6:16
Not in a Place Called Church,
32, 64
Galatians
5:22-23
Fruit Trees, 11, 55
Ephesians
1:7
Blood Disguise, 3, 50
5:27
The Building You Call Church,
7, 52
Philippians
2:8
Obedience the Highest Form of
Praise, 33, 65
Colossians
1:18
The Building You Call Church,
7, 52
II Timothy
2:11
Liar, Liar, 27, 62
2:15
Not in a Place Called Church,
32, 64
Hebrews
5:8
Jesus Learned Obedience, 21,
60

Obedience the Highest Form of
Praise, 33, 65
9:22
Blood Disguise, 3, 50
10:25
Don't Forsake the Assembly, 8,
53
12:1
So Great a Cloud of Witnesses,
39, 69
12:6
Boys Into Men, 5, 51
I Peter
1:23
Holy Rollers, 19, 59
2:9
Holy Rollers, 19, 59
II Peter
2:1-3
Not in a Place Called Church,
32, 64
I John
5:1
Holy Rollers, 19, 59
Revelations
3:19
Boys Into Men, 5, 51
19:7-9
With His Own Blood, 45, 73
21:9
With His Own Blood, 45, 73

www.ingramcontent.com/pod-product-compliance
Lightning Source LLC
Chambersburg PA
CBHW071833020426
42331CB00007B/1709